more money for shoes

A CIP catalogue of this book is available from the National Library of Australia.

Browne, Melissa

More Money For Shoes
ISBN: 978-0-9808097-5-6

Published and Project Managed by The Messenger Group

The Messenger Group
Project & Creative Director: Jade Dunwoody
Illustrations: mekel -- www.mekel.net
Editorial: Lauren Barker & Anthea England
Design: Camilla D'Arcy & Edith Swan

Published by The Messenger Group Pty Ltd
PO Box H241
Australia Square NSW 1215
www.themessengergroup.com.au

this book has been inspired by

the many women that I come in contact with every day – friends, co-workers, colleagues, clients who often place too many limitations on what they're capable of being. I want to show them that business is not just a man's domain. Women have the potential to be incredible, powerful, successful business owners – if only they embrace all of business and not simply the warm, fuzzy parts. After all, if a woman can negotiate cobbled back-streets in five-inch heels she can certainly nail the tricky concepts of business.

Thanks to my gorgeous husband, Tony Larven, who offered to illustrate this book with his amazing stick-figures. Maybe next time honey. Xx

contents

MY WARDROBE & YOUR BUSINESS

let me start this book by writing about something very close to my heart: my wardrobe.

I have the most incredible wardrobe. I'm fortunate it's the size of a roomy bedroom, has a ton of drawers, space for a hundred pairs of shoes (my husband wishes I was kidding about that part), long hanging rails, medium hanging rails and on and on. It also comes complete with a full-length mirror and a chandelier. Yes, you read right, a chandelier.

It wasn't always this way. Prior to this, my wardrobe was in multiple bags scattered throughout the house, in different cupboards, spread over floors and in complete disarray. I had no idea what I owned and probably only wore about 20% of what I possessed. I also wasted a huge amount of money buying multiples of the same thing because I would forget that I already owned something similar or simply couldn't find it. Sound familiar?

So what does my fabulous, organised wardrobe have to do with owning a business? Well, I believe building a business is like building a wardrobe. If you're like me, then you won't be inspired by climbing mountains or taming wild bears, but you will be inspired by perfectly fitting jeans, great shoes, access to a talented stylist and a well organised wardrobe (or your own version of control and organisation). In reality though, you're probably in a state of disarray, grabbing whatever is handy, clean and still fits.

You can be like that in business too. I've met so many business owners who are great at what they do but their business is in a state of organised chaos. They've tried a bunch of things but have never properly implemented anything and have ignored the parts they think are too hard. Many simply don't understand how to run a successful and profitable business or feel daunted by the processes involved.

Some well-dressed gals (and blokes) might appear to have a great wardrobe but it's only an illusion – they're racked up to their eyeballs with credit card debt and don't really 'own' any of it. Countless business owners that I've met are the same. They have the façade of a great business but it's barely profitable, they're not paying themselves and there's no money in the bank. That's not having a great business!

It doesn't have to be this way.

I believe every business owner has the potential to have an incredible, successful, profitable business, in the same way every woman has the potential to have an amazing, organised, highly functional wardrobe. In some women's closets will be racks of Gucci, Prada, suits and stilettos, while others will have drawers full of Target, Country Road, flowing dresses and thongs.

It's the same in business. Some women will own multi-million dollar, award-winning companies and others will run incredibly successful home-based businesses. The key is working out what you want your business to be. You need to define your own version of success. This means not taking on the expectations of others and making sure your business not only looks successful from the outside, but is also profitable and running well on the inside.

This book has been designed to show you how to do just that. It's not a textbook for how to run a business – otherwise it would be three times as thick and potentially frighten (or bore) you with tables, graphs and spreadsheets. That wouldn't be helpful because then you'd never find out what you need to know. Instead, its job is to motivate, educate and inspire you to believe that running a successful and profitable business really isn't that hard. Together, we'll look at the important things you should be doing in your business and, just as importantly, why you should be doing those things.

Now educating and inspiring you is great, but what about practical assistance? Well, once you read about a principle that you know is missing in your business or that you need to work on, simply tick which actions you need to take in the To Do Lists at the end of each chapter then make sure you take the time to do those things! If you need more help, I've also included Shopping Lists full of tools, forms, checklists and templates, all of which you can download for free on the More Money for Shoes website (www.moremoneyforshoes.com.au). These handy, downloadable extras will help you put all of those important principles into practise in your business.

Understanding how to run a great business isn't hard. But, like finding the perfect jeans, you do have to put in the legwork. My aim is to show you that building an amazing business is like building a great wardrobe. Together we're going to organise, throw out, build and create. Who knows, you might even be inspired (metaphorically or literally) to hang your own chandelier…

So strap on your stilettos (or ballet flats) and let's have some fun discovering how your business can be more than just an expensive hobby and how you too can have more money for shoes!

"a girl should be two things. classy and fabulous."

Coco Chanel

THE CLEAN UP

moving in together is bliss, right?

When my husband and I first moved in together, we crammed all our belongings into a little rented house. I looked at his things, he looked at my things and we both wondered how we would politely tell the other they had a lot of rubbish they needed to throw out. Being an accountant, I thought I was incredibly savvy not throwing out any of my clothes as I still wore the same size that I did when I left school (please don't hate me – the downside is I still haven't grown boobs). My husband felt a little differently… especially when he figured out I had kept such gems as my year 10 and year 12 formal dresses. What transpired over the following weeks was a grand fashion parade of all my bags of clothing, including a pair of tight, bright green, cropped skinny jeans with zippers down the side, straight from the '90s.

When the dust cleared, I had three large garbage bags filled with clothes I hadn't worn in years, a list of things I needed to purchase and a wardrobe of items I was fairly convinced I would wear over the next 12–18 months. As well as a big headache. I have to admit I dreaded the clean up, but at the end of the long and agonising process, I felt a whole lot better about what was left behind. Plus I could now go shopping, armed with a list of what I needed to really make my wardrobe work for me. Any excuse to go shopping is always a bonus!

As business owners, we need to conduct the same stocktake on ourselves and our businesses. Having been through this process again recently, I found it to be an incredibly emotional and occasionally traumatic experience. Not unlike my wardrobe clean up.

Why do I think a clean up is important? Over the years I have met with hundreds of business owners and I know they are generally great at what they do. They are great architects, doctors, shop owners, online store retailers, product developers and so on. What they are not so great at is being a business owner and running a successful business.

So what can you do? The first step is to remove your head from the big pile of cashmere you have dug it into (cashmere sounds so much better than sand) and admit you need to become skilled at being a business owner. You need to be honest about what skill sets you possess, as well as the skill sets you lack. You also need to look at your business and what is working in it and what isn't.

When I did my clean up, I realised that my business was lacking systems and procedures, my cash flow was terrible, I had staff I needed to move on and as a business owner I was lacking accountability, people skills and a regular pay. That's a long list and some tough things to own up to, but if I hadn't acknowledged them my business would have suffered.

Many of you don't know what's missing in your business because you don't know what you should be doing in the first place. All you know for certain is you could be earning more, you want more options, you want less stress and finally, there's a whole lot you don't know. That's a great place to start.

Some of you may know your weakness is understanding the numbers, financial statements and budgeting (actually, anything to do with accounting) but you've tried to ignore this whole area, hoping you can be fabulous in other parts of your business and it will make up for this lack of financial acumen. Now is a great time to change your mindset and have a crack at grasping something that has always scared or bored you.

A stocktake can be tough because it forces you to get real. It was difficult for me to acknowledge I was never going to wear my tight, bright green, cropped jeans with zippers down the side again. It meant I was leaving my 20s behind. But by acknowledging that they no longer worked for me, it meant I could replace them with a pair of very fabulous, dark, high-waisted skinny jeans that my late-30s self adores.

The first step in becoming a great business owner is acknowledging you have a lot to learn and you're not doing everything right. If you're a perfectionist like me, this can be tough. But once you accept this, you can start planning how you're going to fill in the gaps. That's when the real fun begins and you can take the first brave steps (in gorgeous heels, of course) toward becoming a great business owner and creating an amazing business.

to do list

1. write down up to five skills you lack as a business owner

2. write down five areas of your business you have been ignoring because they're too hard or too boring.

3. make a conscious decision to grab the items above out of the too-hard basket, deal with them and understand them. sometimes just choosing to think differently can make a huge difference.

4. write down five things that are working well within your business and congratulate yourself!

shopping list

- [ ] business owner's reality check

PLANNING

i love planning. I love pulling out my diary and working out what I have on over the next few weeks. It's probably no surprise I ended up as an accountant and business coach as I love things like structure and forecasting. Just writing about it makes me want to start a new list of things to do, plan and achieve.

I'm like this in my private life as well. Sometimes my husband will look at me and say, "Want to do some planning?" He may as well start taking his clothes off, it's so sexy to me.

I think it's clear from the previous chapter I'm a list maker with my wardrobe too. Each spring and autumn I go through my wardrobe and create three piles. One to give away, one to throw away and one to be altered. This means I don't have to wait 20 years for another giant wardrobe clean up as I'm regularly taking stock. I also create a list of what I need that is missing and if that list isn't too long I might add a few items I've had my eye on. Then it's off to the shops!

Now I'm not saying you need to have the same fixation with lists and planning that I do. But, I think it's important to take stock so you know what you have to work with. You also need to know where you are going so you can plan ahead. You don't want to arrive at a party, look around and realise you still have your year 10 formal dress on five or 10 years later, when everyone else has moved on. I've done it. It's not a good look.

In the previous chapter we looked at doing a stocktake on your business, as well as on you as a business owner. Now I want you to think about the future. To take a look in the crystal ball and describe what your business will look like in three years and 10 years time.

I'm talking specifics, such as:

- How many customers will you have?
- What will your yearly sales be?
- How many team members will you have?
- What will the culture be?
- What type of clients will you have?
- How many product lines will you have?
- How many locations will you have?
- What will your profit be or how much will you take out of the business?

Next, we need to think about you as the business owner. So for those same time periods, list:

- What will you look like as a business owner?
- In what capacity will you be involved? E.g. still doing day-to-day work, CEO, other role.
- Will the business be sold and will you simply be a consultant?
- How many hours a week will you be working?
- How many weeks holiday will you be taking each year?
- What awards will you have you won?
- What will you and the business be known for?

Why three years and 10 years? Well, three years is close enough that it feels realistic but far enough away that it's still aspirational. Ten years, however, is your big dream. Jim Collins (the ultimate business stylist) calls this your 'Big Hairy Audacious Goal' or BHAG. This is where you are able to really go crazy and imagine what your business has the potential to look like. For some of you, it might be a business with locations in three states, revenue of $15 million and 25 employees. For others, it will be a business that earns a profit of $200,000 per year with two staff members and you only working four days a week. The most important thing is to find the BHAG that is right for both you and your business.

Not everyone loves lists like me, but you need to know what you want your business to be so that you can work out how you're going to get there. Hoping you will have a business that's successful and gives you a nice lifestyle is not enough. So instead of simply aspiring to be 'successful', think about what sales figure this means or how much profit you want. Instead of 'a nice lifestyle', write down how much money that would take and how often you would be working.

My own BHAG includes revenue in the millions, a six figure annual profit and winning certain awards, including being in BRW's Top 10 Best Places to Work. Are these feasible goals? Only I can answer that and only time will tell. But what I do know through experience is if I stretch myself and aim high, I might not quite reach what I aim for, but I'll usually get very close. That's often much further than I honestly believed I could achieve.

Finally, don't be scared to dream big. In the words of the inspirational Nelson Mandela, "Our deepest fear is not that we are inadequate. Our deepest fear is that we are powerful beyond measure. It is our light, not our darkness that most frightens us. We ask ourselves, 'Who am I to be brilliant, gorgeous, talented and fabulous?' Actually, who are you not to be?" So as you think about where you want to be in three years and 10 years time, dream big colourful dreams and don't be afraid of the fabulous business owner you are capable of becoming!

to-do list

1. make a list of what you want your business to look like in three years time. (refer to the questions above.)
2. make a list of what you will look like as the business owner in three years time. (again, refer to the questions above.)
3. describe your bhag for 10 years time. this may be a bit more vague but it should still be something measurable (e.g. sales figure or number of units sold).

shopping list

- [ ] setting smart goals
- [ ] how to set a BHAG (10 year goal)
- [ ] action plan for goals

BEING TRUE TO YOURSELF

i adore fashion magazines. I consume Vogue on a monthly basis and whet my appetite in between issues with gorgeous fashion blogs. I love movies full of fashion and glamour like The Devil Wears Prada, Breakfast at Tiffany's and The September Issue. It's probably why I fell in love with Sex and the City and Mad Men.

It should come as no surprise then that I love frocking up and going out to dinner, the races or brunch. Like the stylist Rachel Zoe, I'm an advocate for dressing up or wearing your favourite outfit whenever the mood takes you. So, 4-inch heels for brunch down at my local cafe on a Sunday morning? Sure. A wrist full of bangles and a jumpsuit to a family function down the South Coast? Why not? Leather shorts and ankle boots to pick out tiles for a renovation? Absolutely. Maybe it's a reaction against the modern-day obsession with jeans, but I love dressing up.

I haven't always been this way. Particularly in my 20s, it was easier to wear the unofficial uniform of my friends and don the standard jeans and a pretty top when I went out. However, with age (and hopefully wisdom), I began to feel more comfortable in my own skin and experiment with my wardrobe choices. Sure, sometimes I'm overdressed and at times my husband or a girlfriend will cock an eyebrow at what I've chosen. But if I'm happy and confident in my choice then does it really matter? I'm also an admirer of others who are confident with their own style, like the 90-year-old (yes you read right, 90) international style icon and self-described 'geriatric starlet',

Iris Apfel. I love this woman. When asked for style tips she said, "I can't tell people how to have style. No amount of money can buy you style...You have to learn who you are first and that's painful." What I think Mrs Apfel is saying is that we need to find our authentic self. Too often, we try to copy what someone else is wearing or what the current trends are dictating without a thought for whether it suits us or represents who we are. Take a look next time you walk around your local shopping centre – most people dress almost in an unofficial uniform. Mums wear jeans and a t-shirt, teenagers wear jeans and a t-shirt, guys wear jeans and a t-shirt. It's all so very blah.

Many businesses also seem to adopt the unofficial uniform or brand of their profession. Accountants colour everything blue and talk about being proactive, cafés all have smallish square tables, dentists wear white coats and lawyers wear grey suits. If you question the owner on why they chose a colour, used certain words on their website or bought particular furniture for their office, they usually don't have a great explanation. Maybe it was suggested to them, it sounded good or it was cheap.

So what's the alternative and how can you be true to yourself with your business? Well, just as your clothes hint to the world who you are as a person, your business branding should convey what your business does, what you value and should form a connection with your customers. They say when you first meet someone you form an opinion about who they are and what they are like within the first five seconds. Now that may not sound fair but it happens every time. The same is true for your business.

Take a moment to answer the following questions and consider, what that says about who you are as a business owner and what your business stands for:

- What does your website look like and what words are used?
- What do your premises look like?
- What sort of coffee do you serve and how is it served?
- What do your brochures and other promotional materials look like?
- How does your team greet your customers?
- What does your team look like – how do they present themselves to your customers?
- How do you dress and present yourself?

Why is this important? Every time someone interacts with you and your business, they're making a judgement about what you're like as a business and what you value. If you're simply a carbon copy of everyone else in your industry, what will the judgement be? That you're the same as everyone else in your industry – despite what you might actually be doing. Similarly, if you're saying you're an innovative and forward-thinking business but your office looks tired and your people act in an unmotivated manner, do you think your customers will believe you? No, I don't either.

I'm a tall, blonde female in her late 30s (OK it might be 40s by the time of publishing) with a penchant for dressing up and high heels. When I first started out in business I would put my hair in a bun, wear a lot of black and grey – and try hard not to stand out. Fast forward 10 years and I know there are not many female owners of accounting firms and still fewer who are 6-feet tall and blonde. So I actively embrace my uniqueness. How? By choosing to be different in how I look, act and speak, both as a business owner and in my business.

Some examples are:

- Our offices feel warm and professional but are a little different. The North Sydney office has groups of café-style tables, wireless internet for clients to use, lounges and a cowhide rug.
- You'll rarely see me in a suit and almost never in shoes that are under 3-inches.
- My team and I deliberately speak and write in a way that is conversational, friendly and easy to understand. This goes for meetings, client reports and marketing material.
- I write a blog about fashion and business which you can read at www.moremoneyforshoes.com.au. Why hide my two loves?
- I use lots of photos of my team and clients on the website, in newsletters, on photo-boards in my offices, on Christmas cards and in printed photo-books.
- Our corporate colours are red and chocolate brown.

What's important is I know my style, I know who I am and I'm being authentic with that through my business. If you hate glamour, heels and dressing up, then you don't need a wardrobe full of stilettos and party dresses. Similarly, there's a reason why I still don't own a tracksuit – I would simply never wear it! The same applies to your business. It's important to understand your own style and personality and how they may influence what your business is and can be. Many business owners are incredibly interesting people but their business is simply a slightly different version of what everyone else is doing. Instead, why not dare to be different? There's a reason why your customers are attracted to you, so don't hide your personality in your business. As you start to build your business, make the brave decision to create an authentic and extraordinary business. Embrace your uniqueness and start to think about how you might apply your own personal style to your business.

to-do list

1. make a list of 10 things that make you unique.
2. make a list of 10 things that make your business unique.
3. take a good look at your business. if you were a new customer, what would you notice about your office (or home office), your website, your team, your brochures, your product, your reports and so on? are they a reflection of the qualities you listed in points 1 and 2?
4. what are five ways you can improve your business so it stands out and is a reflection of you?

shopping list

☐ review on your business brand

"i'm a woman phenomenally. phenomenal woman that's me."

Maya Angelou

UNDERSTANDING YOUR SHAPE

have you looked in the mirror lately?

I know it sounds like an odd question but it's a question I need to ask you before we go any further. Let me explain why.

One of the first things my husband commented on when we first started dating was my squat legs. Charming, I know. I'm 5"10 and the comment usually made about my legs is that they are long – never that they are squat. But the truth is, he was right. You see I've always known I have a long torso and shorter legs, so I compensate for this with how I dress. Which no doubt explains my heel fetish. The problem is my husband is a physiotherapist so when he stood next to me, he immediately noticed. Drats!

The reason the world is fooled into thinking I have long legs is that I know my body shape and dress accordingly. If I didn't, then I wouldn't know what to hide and what to emphasise. So while I may have shorter legs, I know if I throw on a pair of heels I instantly look like I have the long legs most people think I was born with.

That's why as business owners we need to spend a bit of time getting naked. Now I'm not going to ask you to strip down in front of the mirror. Unless you're like many of the men I know with oodles of self-confidence (or Jen Hawkins), it's just plain mean. But I do want you to take a good look at yourself.

Why bother? Well, so far we've looked at the outside but we haven't looked too hard at the person inside. We've written lists about what we do and don't do as business owners and what we'd like our business to look like, but we've ignored our own strengths and weaknesses. By getting naked (either literally or metaphorically) and truly looking at ourselves, we can acknowledge what we need to focus on and what we need to develop.

As business owners, we need to be really clear about our natural gifts or strengths and start developing and using them. I know you may feel uncomfortable saying you're great at something but you're going to have to get over that. If you're really struggling here then maybe have a colleague, customer or close friend help you with this.

Now if you determine one of your strengths is client relationships and being able to talk their language, then you need to devise ways to get in front of your clients more. If it's creating work and being the rainmaker for your business, then you need to get out and find the work. If it's creating new products and services, then you need to allow time for that. When you figure out what you're naturally talented and gifted at, you can devise a strategy to ensure you're ultimately doing more of that within your business.

As a business owner, you also need to be aware of your weaknesses. Women in particular may be keenly aware of their flaws – they're just not actually doing anything about them. In the same way that I know how to disguise my squat legs, you need to know how to manage your weaknesses. Maybe you're not great at confronting people, managing bookwork, understanding the numbers, creating budgets or developing systems. Instead of ignoring these areas you need a plan to manage them. This might involve reading business books (like this one), going to courses and workshops, or hiring an expert to help you. Ultimately, your weakness may be something you never enjoy and can eventually outsource when your business has the cash flow. However, in the meantime, it's something you need to acknowledge and then actively work on so that your weakness doesn't become a fatal flaw.

One of my own weaknesses is managing and understanding my team. If you're the owner of a growing business with an increasing number of team members, this could potentially be a real problem. Initially I tried to deal with my weakness by ignoring it and concentrating on my clients instead. Not very smart, I know. Ultimately, what I had to do was hire a consultant. That's because the gap between me solving the problem and me being the problem was too wide. The consultant helped me understand I needed to use different methods with different team members rather than just deal with everyone as a whole. It also proved to my team they are valued because I was willing to spend time and resources on them. This has been a great outcome for both me personally and for my business. It was all achieved simply because I acknowledged that I had a weakness.

Getting naked can be tough because it forces you to get real. It's easy to gloss over your strengths and your weaknesses or presume you know what you're dealing with, but it's only when something is openly acknowledged that you can start to manage it. So make a decision to embrace your shape with all of its wonders and imperfections and start being honest about what you have to work with.

to-do list

1. take a seat in front of a mirror, pour a glass of wine if necessary and start getting naked with yourself. write down up to 10 strengths and 10 weaknesses that impact how you behave as a business owner. if you're struggling, grab a good friend to help. look at the list again a few days later and make sure it still feels ok.

shopping list

- [ ] personal swot (strengths weaknesses opportunities threats) analysis

UNDERSTANDING YOUR MARKET

VOGUE

in the fashion magazine world, the largest and most important issue is the September issue. Why? The cynic in me suspects it's the lead up to Christmas so advertisers are keen to push their wares on a cashed up, ready-to-spend public. The fashionista in me doesn't care because she just wants to look at the abundance of pretty pictures.

What's clear to me though, is those in the fashion magazine business have done their research. They know they're not just in the business of creating a magazine but are also in the business of sales and advertising. They know advertisers want to advertise in September (in the run up to Christmas) so they create a special bumper issue that's looked forward to by fashion-loving men and women everywhere.

US Vogue's September issue is always my most anticipated delivery. It's the size of a phone book. Literally. The 2011 September Issue had 758 pages, weighed almost five pounds (almost two kilos) and a documentary was made about its creation. Out of those 758 pages, a whopping 584 were advertisements and due to the high number of ads, the table of contents wasn't completed until page 172. That's a lot of ads!

Now if you asked me to flick through 584 pages of ads, I'd laugh at you. Yet in September 2011, I was delighted to do just that. Why? Because Vogue understands their market. They know their readers, they know their customers (the advertisers) and they've worked out a way to meet both of their needs so that both parties walk away feeling not just satisfied but thrilled with the result. The reader has a large, glamorous magazine and the advertisers are able to not just fill space but create a unique experience for the reader with ads especially designed for the issue. Meanwhile, bloggers, fashion commentators and TV morning show hosts dissect the cover and contents, which creates interest and helps sell more copies of the magazine and more product for the advertisers.Who said fashion folk were dumb? My question to you is do you know your market that well?

If you don't, what can you do to change this? Well, you can start by researching who your customers are, keeping in mind you may have multiple types of customers. Next, find out where they hang out, what social media platforms they use, who they're influenced by, what their buying patterns are and how much money they have to spend. That way you can adapt your product or service to suit.

Some marketers suggest that you actually develop a persona for each customer type. In my business we have two main personas, Tracey and Shannon.

1. Tracey is a female whose partner is in business, so she's in business by default. She is usually a stay-at-home mum who manages the accounts of the business and answers the phones. She spends time on Facebook and socialises with other mums and families.

2. Shannon can be either male or female. He or she is a business owner who actively wants to grow their business. They spend a lot of hours in their business and use social media to make connections. They may or may not have a family, they socialise with close friends and spend time networking with other business owners.

As you can see, these personas are very different, so how we talk, market and tailor products and services to each of them also needs to be very different. The most important thing is we have identified who our customers are and we are actually doing something with that information.

Do you know your customers that well?

Once you know who your customers are, you can work out what they need and adapt your product or service to suit. Or you may work out that you have a number of different customer types but two of them represent 80% of your sales. So what do you do? You might work out how to get the others to spend more with you by tailoring a product for them, marketing differently to them or creating a new product for them. Or you may realise that your two biggest customer types could be spending a whole lot more and so you concentrate on increasing their spend.

Maybe you have something you think is a hard sell – 584 pages of ads certainly is, so take Vogue's lead. Get creative about how you can meet your customers' and suppliers' needs in such a way that everyone is not just satisfied, but thrilled with the result. Once you know who your customers are, then you can take a leaf from the Fashion Bible and find a way to create extraordinary products and experiences for them in your marketplace.

to-do list

1. do you know who your customers are? if not, work out who they are, give them a name, a persona and attributes.
2. what are the unique qualities of your product or service? what can you do better?
3. how are you currently marketing to your customers? does this fit with what you listed in step one or are there other/better ways you can reach your target customers?
4. what percentage of revenue or sales does each customer persona represent?
5. is there a way to increase these percentages or should you be concentrating more on one customer type?

shopping list

- [ ] buying persona template
- [ ] USP review
- [ ] customer spend analysis

BUSINESS

BASICS:

everything you need to know

even though i have a love affair with clothes, shoes and fashion,

I don't always like shopping. Having to navigate the crowds or traipse from store to store with aching feet and enormous blisters from inappropriate heels isn't my idea of fun. (Yes I'm aware these are first world problems, but let's continue anyway.) Now if I said I loved fashion but never actually bought any clothes, it would be a bit of a contradiction. How can you be a fashionista but not actually purchase anything? Sure you might argue you're still researching your style or saving for the perfect pair of shoes but until you actually hang something in your wardrobe, it's just lip service.

The same can be said for business. You might say you want to run a great business, talk about marketing and branding, and pick some funky furniture for your office, but if you're not prepared to actually get involved with the basics of running a business then you're really just playing around.

So what are the basics of running a business? Or your business basics as we'll call them here.

They're the numbers side of your business – those key areas that will influence your profit and bank balance. This is the side of the business so many of my clients try to tell me is too hard, beyond their abilities or not an area they will ever understand.

Well, let me tell you a secret. It's not that hard. Sure, it might not be your forte and you might never love it, but if you want to run a successful, profitable business you can't afford to ignore the basics.

So many things in life are simply a mindset. If you decide you'll never be a great businessperson or a numbers person, then guess what? You'll probably be right. It doesn't help your business though, does it? Imagine instead if you decided to try and understand business and make sense of the numbers? Sure, you may never become an accountant but I guarantee you'll become a much better business owner.

The following nine chapters cover the business basics. To make it a bit of fun and prove anyone can understand the numbers, I've compared each business basic to a wardrobe staple. That's because I believe if you can build a fabulous, stylish, functional wardrobe, then you can certainly build a fabulous, stylish, functional, profitable business. We'll work through them one by one and then it's up to you to tick off the To Do List, head to www.moremoneyforshoes.com.au and download your free Shopping List and apply the principles to your business.

Are you ready? Then roll up your sleeves, put on some bejewelled flats, take a deep breath and let's get started!

BUSINESS BASICS:

sparse & good foundations

i have a confession to make.

I wear Spanx. For anyone who's never heard of Spanx, they're like a longer, higher version of Bridget Jones' mummy undies. Think really, really thick stockings in the style of high-waisted (I'm talking way up on your ribs high) bike shorts or skirts.

So very unattractive.

They are, however, incredibly necessary undergarments. If you're wearing a silk dress that clings and shows every bump, bra and underwear line, then Spanx will smooth all this out so there are no lines and ridges. They're also genius for white dresses, white pants, white jumpsuits, white anything. A bonus for those of us over 35 is they also lift anything that needs lifting.

Now they're not everyday underwear – it's way too much work getting them on and navigating trips to the bathroom. And did I mention how unattractive they are? Instead, they're the bi-weekly or the as-the-outfit-requires-it underwear.

So what does a pair of Spanx have to do with your business?

Foundation underwear may seem unnecessary, but they're always going to make your clothes fit and fall so much better. In the same way, the foundation work in your business is also potentially boring and unappealing (unless you're an accountant), but it's also incredibly necessary to help your business achieve its full potential. So what's the business version of Spanx? They're the foundation plans that you lay

– the business plan and budget. These may seem like seriously unsexy documents but without them you have no basis for what you're doing in your business. You don't know where you're going, what you want to be, what your purpose is, who your customer is, how much money you need and how much money you can make from this business.

Maybe you created one of these documents when you first started out and have never referred to it since. That's about as useful as me buying a pair of Spanx, putting them in my underwear drawer and never actually wearing them. Or maybe you thought about creating a business plan and budget but it all just seemed too hard. That's like Kate Hudson walking the red carpet in a gorgeous gown with serious VPL (visible panty line, for the uninitiated). Her stylist would never let her get out of the car because her ridiculously expensive dress would appear very ordinary.

In the same way I don't don my Spanx every day, you won't revisit your foundation documents every day. I suspect if you did, it would be a waste of time and resources. Weekly, fortnightly or monthly, however, is a must. It's such a great waste of time having your business looking amazing only to see it come undone by failing to create and regularly referring to your foundation documents. If you think it all sounds too hard, let me start by dispelling some myths.

Firstly, a business plan does not need to be a 50-page document. Instead, the most successful plans are succinct and contain only the information you really need to know. For example, I believe 12 pages is plenty. If even that sounds like too much, there are some talented designers (such as 'The Growth Guy', Verne Harnish) who have created one-page plans. Sure, there's work involved in completing these one-page plans but once you do it's simply a matter of tweaking them every quarter. I use Verne's one-page plan with great success in my own business because I can pin it on my wall. In fact, everyone in my business has it at their desks and it serves as a daily reminder of what we stand for and where we're going.

Secondly, your budget doesn't have to be perfect and you don't have to be an accountant to create one. (Don't tell your accountant I said that, but it's true.) A budget can be a starting point. Some of the figures within it won't be right but you can update it during the year as you get more clarity on what your real costs are. A budget shouldn't be a static document. Instead, it should be a living thing you refer to each month (at least) to see how your business is going. If you use accounting software, and you should, you can enter your budget and print reports to compare how you're really going. It's that simple.

The great thing about a budget is it also prepares you for any 'holes' that might come up during the year and allows you to prepare for them in advance. For example, I shut my offices for three weeks over Christmas and during this time there's no income but the expenses just keep on coming. By preparing a budget each year, I know how big the hole is going to be and I can make sure I have money put aside for it. If the thought of preparing one of these documents makes you break out in a sweat, then just like there are stylists for clothes, there are also professionals who can assist you with creating business plans and budgets. Maybe seek out professional help for your first one and then you should be fine to tweak it yourself after that.

Like great supportive underwear, you need to ensure your business is supported from the very beginning. Make sure you're the good friend who grabs your business before it walks out of the door with VPL. Sure it's not sexy or exciting but it's important to take the time to create a business plan and budget that will make your business look amazing and show off its full potential.

to-do list

1. put time aside to prepare a business plan and budget for your business.
2. if you already have a business plan and haven't looked at it in the last six months, then pull it out and refresh it.
3. if you already have a budget but haven't done anything with it, then enter it into your accounting program and run monthly reports to track how you are going.

shopping list

- [ ] budget template and step-by-step guide
- [ ] comparison of accounting software table
- [ ] business plan template and instruction guide
- [ ] information on verne harnish's method and his one page plan
- [ ] action plan for business plan
- [ ] action plan for budget

BUSINESS BASICS:

the white shirt & business systems

it should come as no surprise to discover I have more than one white shirt. I also have multiple white t-shirts and white singlets. Actually, due to the number of these I own, I'm fairly convinced they're breeding in my closet.

Now I know the white shirt is not the most glamorous item in your wardrobe. I don't think I've ever received a compliment on my gorgeous white shirt. That's because it's not a 'wow' item – a classic often isn't. Having said that, think back to these classic white shirt moments:

- Paired with black pants: Uma Thurman in Pulp Fiction
- Teamed with a long skirt: Audrey Hepburn in Roman Holiday
- Worn with a ball gown: Sharon Stone on the red carpet
- Covering up a bad outfit: Julia Roberts in Pretty Woman

When you think of those women in those outfits in those moments, anything else just seems wrong. A more glamorous option would detract from the moment. Instead, the classic white shirt shines. It becomes the bones of the outfit, of the look, of the moment. Its simplicity allows the moment to be built around it.

So what are the bones of your business? What's the classic your business is built around?

I think the white shirt in your business is its systems and procedures. On their own, systems and procedures seem boring, ordinary and decidedly unsexy. But when teamed with great staff, vision, budgets and marketing, they become the backbone of your business. Good systems and procedures make your staff shine and your business hum along seamlessly. Most days any way.

I'm reluctant to use McDonald's as an example but they are the textbook case study of systems used incredibly well. They're the perfect case of the white shirt in action (albeit a large, cheap one that I'm fairly sure would be polyester). After all, what other business could leave an 18-year-old manager in charge of a busy store with lots of younger team members and be confident everything will run like clockwork? Think of any franchise for that matter. Often the only difference between a franchise and the business down the road are the systems and procedures that come with it.

Without systems, your business can end up lurching along, hoping for the best. Remove systems and your business is reliant on the mood and work ethic of your people. While that may work for a while with some great team members, it won't be OK in the long run. Inconsistencies would start creeping in. Team members would answer the phone however they liked, customers would be served in assorted ways (some good, some bad) depending on who was serving them and your business wouldn't be able to guarantee a consistently great experience. And customers generally vote with their feet – by walking out of your business and into your competitor's to see if they're doing a better job.

Good systems and processes will always make things easier for both you and your team members. People are often surprised by the small number of team members I have, but I know I can do more with less because we have great systems.

Let me give you two examples from my business:

1. In a traditional accounting firm, the accountant will pick up a job, hope all of the client's information is there and then have to put it back down when they realise things are missing. They chase the client for the missing information (often a number of times), call the client to make an appointment at the end of the job and print the necessary reports. Seems logical, but the problem is the client is being charged for the time it takes the accountant to perform these administrative tasks and it's a waste of time when the accountant could be getting other work done.

So we created systems in our business so our admin team could perform these tasks instead of the accountants. Sure, it took a bit of time initially to create the systems and train the admin team, but now it's completely worth it.

2. I also created a unique process called the Tax Month System for our workflow process, which is a critical part of our business. Clients are allocated a tax month in May and then four weeks before their month they are sent a fixed price agreement, checklists questionnaires and are guaranteed their work will be completed by the end of that month.

If they don't bring their work in on time, my CSA (client services assistant) begins a series of reminders. We also guarantee individual clients that their work will be completed within 10 days. We're obviously under a lot of pressure to deliver results but this entire workflow system is run seamlessly by our 19-year-old CSA, Hannah.

The reason I trust Hannah to make sure there's enough work coming into our business and that the work is completed on time is because she follows a great system. This system includes step-by-step procedures, forms, templates – the whole shebang. But it's simple enough that she can take it and run with it. My team have also tweaked and improved my Tax Month System along the way. Was I offended? Absolutely not. I love that they took ownership of the system and wanted to perfect it. It's all about creating systems, enabling your team members and then letting go.

If it's just you doing the work you might think, why bother?

Well, by creating good systems now it means when your first team member walks in the door, your life will be so much easier. If I had my time again, I would spend much more time doing this while I was still building the business to remove headaches later on. It also means you should be more effective because you'll have worked out and documented the best way of doing things. This will mean happier customers, a happier team, less stressed business owners and ultimately, more cash.

It doesn't matter what type of industry you're in or what your business looks like. Whether you're the Uma, Audrey, Sharon or Julia of your industry, documented systems and procedures should always be a basic, can't-live-without item. Don't leave the running of your business to chance – make it a true classic by investing in the basics.

Of course the style of your white shirt, like your systems and procedures, is entirely up to you.

to-do list

1. review your written (preferably online) systems and procedures to make sure they'e still relevant.
2. if your systems are untested, ask someone else to come in and try to follow them to make sure they're user-friendly.
3. create systems and procedures for every area of your business, from how to answer your phones, to how to process a customer order, through to how to lock up at night.

shopping list

- [ ] systems checklist
- [ ] step-by-step guide to creating systems
- [ ] workflow template
- [ ] action plan for processes

"i've always thought of the t-shirt as the alpha and omega of the fashion alphabet."

Giorgio Armani

BUSINESS BASICS:
the little black dress & cash flow

every woman should have an lbd

(little black dress) – a go-to dress you can rely on in case you need to get ready in a hurry, you're having a bad hair day, you're having an I-feel-fat day or you simply can't be bothered to be creative with your outfit.

The classic LBD isn't necessarily a showstopper, sexy or glamorous (although it certainly can be). Instead it's the safe option. The LBD isn't a 'wow' outfit but it's one of those staples you simply can't do without. Kind of like your best girlfriend – safe, trustworthy and reliable. Sometimes a girl needs that.

In your business, the LBD is money in the bank, or cash flow. It's a strange thing to say but sometimes even the most successful businesses go broke because there's no money in the bank. Profits and revenue can be stars but until the money starts rolling in, your business can still fail.

Don't believe me? Say a business has sales of $5 million – sounds like a successful business doesn't it? But if it isn't pricing its goods or services appropriately or is taking a long time to fulfil orders and then longer again to get paid, then it will go broke very quickly. Why? There's no cash, or not enough cash, coming in to run the business.

Suddenly the LBD is looking very sexy, isn't it? That's because without cash you can't survive. Without cash, you can't pay your team, your suppliers, your rent or yourself.

So how do you make sure you have good cash flow in your business? Well, you can start with the following 10 actions:

1. Have strong terms of trade with your customers.
2. Invoice quickly.
3. Create systems.
4. Create efficiencies so sales (or jobs) are completed faster.
5. Have and use cash flow budgets so you can plan for problems or low sales periods.
6. Use good debtor collection systems.
7. Maintain great relationships with your customers.
8. Maintain great relationships with your bank.
9. Understand how long it takes for you to get paid.
10. Ask for money up front.

Let's look at a couple of these. Number two seems like an obvious one, doesn't it? Wouldn't you want to invoice quickly? You'd think so, but so many businesses don't. Consider the plumber who turns up, does the job and then posts the invoice when he gets home instead of writing or emailing it on the spot. Or the accounting firm that invoices at the end of every month instead of as soon as the job is complete. Both are examples of not sending out invoices as quickly as possible, which means customers will take longer to pay and the business' cash flow is affected.

Number 10, on the other hand, seems a bit cheeky. Surely you can't ask for money before you do the job? Well, why not? You might not always be able to ask for the whole amount, but what about asking for a deposit before you start or offering a small discount if customers pay at the start of a job? It's often the business owner's self-confidence that stops them from asking for money up front or the fact that no one else in your industry does it. That's not a good enough excuse. In my industry, accountants generally give you a bill when they've finished your work, but at my firm we give a fixed price up front and ask for a 50% deposit before we start the job. The fixed price gives clients certainty so they don't mind parting with 50% upfront. My advice? Don't worry about what the rest of your industry is doing. If you can find a way of doing things so your clients are happy and you're being paid ahead of time, just do it.

Be creative with your cash flow and how you're paid. Just like there are hundreds of versions of the LBD, there will be many ways you can control cash flow in your business. Like the LBD, it's not a one-size-fits-all approach. Sometimes it will involve you trying a few different things on for size and seeing how they fit. Not everything will work but don't let that scare you from having another go.

Cash flow, like the LBD, doesn't sound particularly glamorous but it will make your life easier. I'm not a big fan of uniforms or a prolific wearer of the LBD, but sometimes you just need a safe option. In your business you might not be a fan of systems, efficiencies, finance or budgets, but I bet you're a big fan of money in the bank.

to-do list

1. read through the 10 cash flow tips listed above.
2. for those that you are already doing, re-evaluate whether you can do them better.
3. for those that you are not doing, make a list of what needs to be done, by who and when.

shopping list

- ☐ cash improvement strategies
- ☐ debt collection systems
- ☐ cash flow budget template and instructions
- ☐ action plan for cash flow management

BUSINESS BASICS:

handbags & capacity

at the moment i have five large handbags on rotation. They're all large enough that I spend a fair amount of time fishing for keys at the bottom and every day I transfer the contents from one bag to another. I know it would be infinitely more sensible and less time consuming to only have one bag… but that's never going to happen. So I have a system to transfer my belongings between bags instead.

This is essentially a number of small pouches that contain necessary items such as make-up, business cards, vouchers and of course my wallet. I simply move these pouches when I change bags instead of having everything loose at the bottom and leaving something behind.

Even though my everyday handbags are large, they're only ever about one-third full. That's because I doubt I could carry them all day if they were full without incurring some sort of serious shoulder injury. Not a good look!

You may be thinking, 'What does this daily bag dilemma have to do with my business?' Well, just like I decide on a daily basis what size bag to carry, what colour it should be, how much to fill it, what needs to be transferred and whether I can get away with a clutch, you need to decide on the volume and capacity that's appropriate for your business.

What do I mean by volume and capacity? Essentially this is how much product you're able to make or buy, or how much time you have available to deliver your services.

These may seem like basic things you should know but so many business owners don't. So how do you work out what your capacity is?

This involves asking yourself some key questions:

1. If I'm a service-based business:

- How many hours are available to deliver our service?
- Are there some functions a non-fee earner can do so more hours are available?

2. If I'm a product-based business:

- If I'm manufacturing, how many units of product can my machinery make in an hour? How many hours are available?
- Are there any processes I can implement that will increase this?
- How much will the materials or stock cost and how much can I afford to finance?
- If it's a handmade item, how many units of product can my team make in an hour? How many hours are available?

At this stage, you're not interested in pricing, costs or anything like that, you just want to find out how much is possible. For example, if you look at your machinery and work out the most you can make is 50,000 units of product a year, there's no point doing the sums in later chapters with 100,000 units (unless you're intending to purchase another machine). Similarly, if you receive an order of 80,000 units, you would need to work out if you would still make a profit by purchasing a machine or leasing a machine because as it stands today, you can't fill that order.

Why bother working out your volume and capacity? Because it helps with your planning. Yes, there's that word I love again. By working out what you're capable of producing, stocking or servicing, you can then work out what your costs and your profit will be, rework your sales price if necessary to make sure you have a profit and then go out and find your customers. It also helps you work out at what point you'll need more team members or machinery.

Let me break it down with an example. Let's say Jane runs a marketing business. At the moment, the team includes Jane, a receptionist and another marketer. Jane works out she has 50% of her time available to charge out to clients or 18.75 hours per week, her fee-earner has 80% or 30 hours per week and her receptionist has five hours. Jane now knows she has 53.75 hours per week available to do the work. Next, she needs to work out how long an average job will take and determine how many clients she's able to take on. So if she works out she can service 100 clients, then she has a starting point in terms of how many clients she needs. By knowing her capacity, she can make sure these clients will pay her costs and provide her with the profit she wants.

But let's say Jane only wanted to work a 20-hour week. Then she would simply adjust her capacity to suit. This might mean less clients or hiring a part-time fee-earner so Jane can reduce her hours. She might also choose to only work with 80 clients but charge a premium for those clients and allow them to take up more time. That's great. At least she has a starting point to work out what she's capable of doing and what she wants to do.

Like my handbags, you will probably never fill your capacity or volume to the brim. That's because machines need to be serviced, staff need to be trained, internal meetings need to be held, networking events need to be attended and a whole host of other things that take up your time during the day. Once your volume and capacity are set though, you need to track this to make sure your machinery and your staff are working at their optimum capacity. If they're not, then look at why. Maybe team members need to be trained in processes or taught time management techniques, or equipment needs to be upgraded.

In my business, my aim is not to spend any more than 30% of my time doing chargeable work. That leaves me time to train, plan, create new products and services, and meet with my clients. As a business owner, sometimes it's important to reduce the time you spend as a fee-earner. You may not be able to do this straight away, particularly if it's just you, but it can be something you work towards as you build up your business.

Just like I have determined that my favourite handbags look their best when they're one-third full, make sure you work out the optimum capacity for your business. That way you can ensure your business is reaching its full potential, looking its best and performing as profitably as it can be – which of course means more money in the bank for you.

to-do list

1. answer the key questions above.
2. use your answers to work out a plan to fill up your capacity.
3. if your capacity is full, then work out a plan for putting on your next team member or piece of equipment.
4. educate your team on their expected capacity and monitor it regularly.

shopping list

- [ ] volume and capacity calculator
- [ ] action plan for volume and capacity

"i'm thinking balls are to men, what purses are to women. it's just a little bag but we'd feel naked in public without it."

Carrie Bradshaw (Sex and the City)

BUSINESS BASICS:

the two-piece suit & costs

so by now you know i have squat legs, a long torso and no boobs. Too much information, I'm sure. Anyway, like most women, I'm also not the same size up top as down the bottom. And because of this, I'm so thankful for the person who decided (very sensibly) to sell separates for everything from bikinis through to suits!

Being an accountant, you'd think I'd wear a lot of suits. Thankfully that's not the case but the ones I do own, as you may suspect by now, are a little different. White and cream are favourites, as are the floral variety that appeared down the runway in the last few seasons. I also don't always wear the jacket and pants together. Instead, I'll wear the jackets with jeans or shorts and the pants with silk blouses. Suits can give you tons of options so the savvy shopper in me loves them.

When I think of suits and your business, I think of costs. Why? Well, just like a suit has two pieces, within your business you also have two sets of costs. These are your direct costs (we'll call them your suit jackets) and your fixed costs (or your suit pants). Just like I can separate my jacket from my pants, I can separate these costs and consider them independently. So what's the difference between the two costs and why do you need to know about them?

Your direct costs are how much it costs you to make your product or produce your service. This might include materials, packaging, distribution and factory labour, or for services this might simply be labour. Your fixed costs are the costs you have regardless of whether you do or sell anything. They include rent, electricity, phones, bank charges, accounting, stationery, postage, insurance, some labour and interest. You should be able to break these costs down so you know how much it costs to make each unit of product or each hour of service. Now I know we're talking dollars, so let me give you an example.

Say you're making 100,000 units of product. You work out your direct costs by adding up your materials, packaging, factory labour and distribution (and any other costs of production). In our example let's imagine when we add up these costs they total $1 million. If you break this down to each individual unit, you can work out it costs $10 to make each unit of product sold. (Total direct costs divided by the number of units.) Still with me? Good.

Now, does that mean you can sell each unit of product for $11 and make $1 profit? No, it doesn't, because all you've done so far is put on your suit jacket. You haven't put on your suit pants yet, or your fixed costs. So let's say we add up the rest of your costs and they come to $100,000. That means if you make 100,000 units of product, then your fixed cost per unit is $1. (Again, fixed costs divided by number of units.) That means if you sold your product for $11, your profit would be zero. Definitely not a good result!

For service-based businesses, it's a very similar formula. If you know you have five income-earners, a receptionist and a whole lot of expenses, then you simply work out what your average hourly cost is. For example, if your total cost for the year for all of the above is $250,000 and your office hours available are 1,950 hours, then your hourly cost of doing business is $128.21. That means your business needs to make more than $128.21 per hour to make a profit. If you have five earners, then you can break it down per earner so the total cost they each need to recoup per hour is $25.64. Of course this is to cover costs only. We also need to add the amount of profit you want to make.

Now the nice part about fixed costs is it doesn't matter how many units you sell or services you deliver, these costs remain relatively the same. That means in our first example, if you ended up selling 200,000 units of product, your fixed cost per unit would actually drop from $1 to 50c. The same goes for service-based businesses. If you create great efficiencies within your organisation or can sell a service for more money, then your costs won't increase but you'll end up with more money in your bank account. That's a great result.

If you look at direct costs and ignore fixed costs, or vice-versa, then you'll end up with either the suit jacket or the pants. One half of your body will feel very chilly and no doubt you'll receive some strange looks in the boardroom. That's why you need to understand both elements of your costs so you end up with an amazing, perfectly- fitting suit.

Sometimes when you add up your costs it can be a little frightening. Eye-watering even. But it's essential to know this number so you can start to deal with it. Sometimes when you add up the cost of producing a product or service and compare this to the price you can charge, you realise you're actually making a loss on it. In that case, you need to ask yourself some important questions to help you decide whether you should keep making that product or providing that service.

Questions like:

1. Will selling more of your product or service bring your costs down enough so you'll make a profit?

2. If not, can you increase your prices enough so you do make a profit?

3. Is keeping this product or service a strategy so customers are moved quickly into a more expensive and profitable product or service – perhaps one they would not jump into directly?

If you answer no to any of the above questions then you simply have to discontinue your product or service. Or, to put it another way, you need to discard the out-of-date, ill-fitting, full-of-holes suit.

Again, if calculating these numbers is difficult then find an expert to help you. After that, you should be able to keep track yourself.

It's important you know how much it costs you to do business. You can't price your service or product, or work out your profit, until you know this. So grab your suit jacket, slip on your suit pants and start to determine the perfect-fitting suit for your business.

to-do list

1. work out what your total fixed costs are.
2. work out what your variable costs per unit are.
3. determine your product cost or hourly rate.

shopping list

- [ ] analysis of fixed costs and step-by-step guide
- [ ] analysis of direct/variable costs and step-by-step guide
- [ ] how to calculate your break-even point

"i like being a woman, even in a man's world. after all, men can't wear dresses, but we can wear the pants."

Whitney Houston

BUSINESS BASICS:

jeans and pricing

like many women, i struggle shopping for jeans. Maybe it's because I don't have legs that are shaped like sticks, but I find the process of buying jeans a little traumatic.

When I do find the inner strength to embark on a jean hunt, I invariably find myself sitting on the change room floor, sweating, as I struggle to pull a pair of jeans up and over my legs while they attempt to grab my thigh and ankle muscles and slowly strangle them. It's my strong opinion that alcohol should be served in jean stores. It just seems necessary.

When I discovered Sass and Bide jeans many years ago and worked out they had a range that worked for me, I became an instant devotee. Because of this, I know if they put their price up I'd still be a convert.

My mum, however, is a completely different story. If she wears denim it will generally cost less than $80 and will simply be comfortable. My husband on the other hand will pay up to $150 and wants his jeans to look good, but not like he's trying to look like an 18-year-old. Another male friend has no problem with forking out up to $500 for a pair of jeans that are fashion forward, while one of the girls at my office owns no denim but will pay under $50 for jeggings (jean leggings, yes I don't understand them either).

So what does this jean breakdown have to do with your business? Well, my guess is for the most part, the material cost (that is, the denim) is very similar among all of these examples. However, the prices range from under $500 through to $500. So how do the companies that charge $500 get away with it?

Simple. It's because they know their market, they've done their research and they have truckloads of self-belief.

So what about you? Do you belong at the $50 end, the $500 end, or somewhere in the middle? Where does a business owner even start when they're setting a price? I think there are six things you need to consider:

1. Cost: If you've read the Suit chapter you should be able to determine your cost per unit or per hour of service.
2. Your competitors: Is there anyone else doing what you are doing? What are they charging? This is where the inner snoop in you is allowed to come to the surface.
3. Your customers: By now you should have an idea of who it is that will be buying from you. If not, then head back to Understanding Your Market.
4. Your product or service: You need to understand the impact of a change in price. For example, if Tip Top increased the price of their white bread by 5c, they may lose a large number of customers due to a market crowded with an identical product. On the other hand, I strongly suspect if Louis Vuitton increased their handbags by $500, they wouldn't lose a single client.
5. Your positioning: Do you want to be the Christian Louboutin or the Nine West of your marketplace?
6. Your profit: How much profit do you want to make? (A fairly important question but one that is often forgotten.)

All this sounds great in theory, but from my experience there are usually only two things that ultimately determine what price business owners set for their product. That is, their feelings of self-worth and their levels of courage. I think it takes a mountain of self-worth and courage to charge $500 for a pair of jeans. But some business owners clearly have it in bucketloads.

So, what's your self-belief like? What value do you place on your time and what you're selling? Because in my experience, I find the value a business owner places on their product or service is usually a reflection of their own self-belief and often has very little to do with the marketplace. So if you think self-belief is affecting your pricing, then take another look at what you're charging and consider whether you can increase the price for your own products and services. If you're not sure, then ask a customer (or a sample of them) or a trusted business advisor. If you don't think you can charge more, then think about how you can add value. Or think about how you can sell the value of what you're already doing so your customers are willing to pay more.

At the end of the day, there's no correct price. Could the same pair of jeans be sold for $600 instead of $500? Who knows? Until you trial something you simply won't know because pricing isn't an exact science. Instead, it's about knowing your market, knowing your costs, knowing what profit you want to make, believing in yourself and having a go. You won't get it right every time but the more you get to know your market, the more times you'll get pretty close.

A final warning on pricing: If you put up your price you will potentially lose some customers. But sometimes that's OK. Let me tell you a story to explain. I have a client who we'll call Bec. For years Bec didn't make any money from her business and last year she finally put up her prices by 25%. Bec came to see me a year later and was thrilled because the business went from no profit to a $50,000 profit in 12 months. But then Bec said something strange, "Of course, the business isn't doing as well. We've lost customers because you made me put my prices up." Once I picked myself up from the floor, I explained to Bec why this wasn't the case. The problem was she was focusing on how many customers she'd lost and not the fact she now had no credit card debt. Sure Bec had fewer customers, but this meant she could work with fewer staff. So fewer customers, higher prices and fewer staff now meant a profit.

Don't be deterred by the fact you might lose some customers. That's because if you lose a small amount of customers you'll probably still be better off. What you must do, however, is monitor what's happening when you put up your price and understand your market.

Like the search for the perfect pair of jeans, determining the right price will involve some legwork. And just like your favourite jeans will inevitably fall apart over time, your price strategies won't be something that are set forever. But if you put in the effort, I promise you the results (more profit and more money in your bank account) will be worth it.

to-do list

1. review your current pricing structure.
2. snoop to see what your competitors are charging.
3. work out who the buyers are in your business.
4. tell yourself daily that you're worth it.

shopping list

- [ ] pricing review
- [ ] the effect of a discount
- [ ] pricing action plan

"i have often said that i wish i had invented blue jeans: the most spectacular, the most practical, the most relaxed and nonchalant. they have expression, modesty, sex appeal, simplicity - all i hope for in my clothes."

Yves Saint Laurent

BUSINESS BASICS:
cashmere & efficiencies

in my opinion, there are only a few good things about winter.

These include an open fireplace, red wine, the opportunity to bust out your leather gloves and cashmere.

I used to hate winter. I could never get warm and used to be in a perpetual, mind-numbing, shivering state for the four months or so it took for the sun to kick in again. I used to feel like the Michelin man for most of winter. You know what I mean – having to wear so many bulky layers that you feel if you fell over you would simply roll down the street. That is, until I discovered the joy that is cashmere. Cashmere means you can wear light, gorgeous layers and still feel stylish but most importantly, warm. So incredibly warm.

For me, it's the most efficient item you can have in your wardrobe. It takes up no space at all when you're travelling (this is very important for a serial over packer like me), it's light, warm and functional. But best of all, it's so soft and heavenly that you'll end up stroking your arm and singing soft kitty. Try not to, it can be embarrassing.

In your business, efficiencies are always important. I'm not talking cashmere here but rather the efficiencies that can be gained through improving your workflow or job cycles. Why is that important? Just like I can look and feel like the Michelin man if I'm wearing bulky fibres, you can end up being heavy and cumbersome in your business.

How? Because generally the team members of a business will do things the way they think is best, rather than the smartest and quickest way. By streamlining how team members perform their tasks and even allocating different steps to different team members, you can save time and end up with more money in your bank account.

Don't believe me? Well let's imagine that by creating efficiencies in my business, a job that normally takes eight hours now only takes me six. That means I have two spare hours a day in which to fit more work in. That means I can take on more clients and make more money in one day without adding any extra labour costs. And because I price up front for jobs, I'm rewarded for my efficiencies by being able to keep the extra income. That's certainly an incentive to work smarter!

You can apply efficiencies to any type of business and to just about any function of your business. Some examples are a retailer having a process for ordering stock, a mechanic having a process for servicing a car, a jewellery maker updating their machinery and training staff to shorten production times, or an online retailer creating processes to ensure shorter delivery times. Sounds great in theory, but where do you start?

I find it easier to break it down into seven steps:

1. Divide your business into the different things you do. For example, different product lines or different services you offer.
2. Break each product or service you do into steps. For example, in my business we know completing a business tax return takes 18 steps.
3. Look at each step and ask yourself (and your team) the following questions:
    - Who currently does this step and could someone else do it cheaper (or faster)?
    - Can you do this better?
    - Do you need to do this step at all?
    - Are mistakes being made here?
    - Is it taking longer than it should and is it being double handled?
    - Could you do it differently?
    - Is there equipment available which would do this step better or faster?
4. If you determine you need to rework or reassign steps, now is the time to do it.
5. Assign a team member/s to each step. (If it's just you at the moment, then your name will be on every step but over time this will change.)
6. Create systems and processes for each step and train team members in the new systems.
7. Test and measure the systems to make sure they're working.

Don't be afraid to be creative when you're going through these steps. Take a look at what other industries or businesses are doing for inspiration and please press delete on the recording in your head that says, "But that's the way it has always been done," or, "That would never work in my business." It's your business – that means you can design it the way that works best for your clients, your team and you.

Creating efficiencies in your business is the easiest way to put more money in your bank account. By shortening the time it takes you to do things, you can do more with the same number, or fewer, resources. This is kind of like going from a big, chunky, nylon pullover that really doesn't keep you warm to a thinner, more fashionable, softer and incredibly warm cashmere throw. Both will do the job but one simply does it a whole lot better and gives you a much better result.

More for less. Don't we all want that? Well, by spending the time working out ways you and your team can be more efficient in your business, you'll achieve just that.

to-do list

1. review your efficiencies for your products and services.
2. follow the steps 1-7 above for each product and service in your business.

shopping list

- ☐ efficiency review
- ☐ efficiency cost saving guide
- ☐ workflow or job flow template
- ☐ efficiency action plan

"i wanted to give a woman comfortable clothes that would flow with her body. a woman is closest to being naked when she is well-dressed."

Coco Chanel

BUSINESS BASICS:
the trench & critical numbers

if there is a critical item every wardrobe needs, it must be the trench.

For me, there's so much functionality in a trench and yet so much potential drama. Who knew you could have both in the one item?

The trench is one of those items that it doesn't matter if you're male or female, short or tall, skinny or not-so-skinny, it simply works. And the theatre! Just think of Humphrey Bogart in a classic trench in Casablanca or Audrey Hepburn and George Peppard kissing in the rain in matching trenches in Breakfast at Tiffany's. It's the perfect item in the perfect moment. Of course, there's also the moment in so many movies when the vixen turns up in a trench coat. With very little underneath. Again, drama.

In everyday life though, the trench is a wardrobe staple. It's functional and designed to be worn over your outfit to protect it from the weather. I think it would have to be really cold for you to wear a trench during dinner. Instead, its role is to protect and maintain your outfit on the way to your destination. Stylishly, of course.

So what is the trench in your business? I think trenches are your critical numbers or key performance indicators. Used correctly, these numbers will protect your business and help it to arrive successfully at the destination you have mapped out for it.

But what are critical numbers and how do you work them out? Critical numbers or key performance indicators are fancy names for a very simple concept. I like the term 'critical number' because I think it describes exactly what it is: the critical number (or numbers) that need to be met in order to achieve your business goals. If you're far away from your critical numbers then your business could end up in trouble. See, functionality and drama – just like a trench.

Critical number/s could be:

- $150,000 in sales this quarter – revenue is often the simplest critical number to track.
- Gross profit of $75,000 – gross profit is simply the sales less your direct costs.
- Wages to be no more than the greater of $50,000 or 33% of sales.
- Stock on hand (or inventory) of no more than $25,000.
- Two patients to be seen by every physician per hour.
- Under 10 days to deliver a service.
- 500,000 units of products sold this quarter.
- 150 new customers this quarter.
- Production time of two minutes per unit.

The critical number/s represent the biggest issue you have in your business at the moment. Here are a few critical numbers some of our clients have used as well as a couple from my own business:

- For my business: Sales per quarter and usually one other number. For example, in the December 2011 quarter, that other number was the number of filing cabinets to be scanned.
- For a new mobile mechanic business: Revenue and number of new clients.

- For a retail shop with stock issues: Total inventory, purchases and sales per quarter.
- For a consulting business struggling with customers paying: Number of A-class clients and debtors to be under 30 days.
- For a café: Cost of plate (food) and wages.

If you aren't sure what to track in your business there are a number of things you can do. If your business fits one of the scenarios above, you can start with those as your numbers or you can head to the items in our Shopping List below for more ideas. If you want be more specific, you can search for benchmark reports for your particular industry. These reports simply describe the results others in your field are achieving. But be warned – sometimes the bar is not set very high, so use these guides as a starting point only. Of course, if it all seems too hard, you can always call in an expert to help you determine what these critical numbers should be.

How often do you need to track your critical numbers? In my business, I track them daily. Yes, daily. That's because I want to grow quickly and it's important that the numbers keep us on track. Sure, some weeks the critical numbers might stay the same for a few days, but I track them daily regardless. At the very least, you should track your critical numbers weekly. Any longer and by the time you react it might be too late. That's also the reason why you should have no more than three critical numbers. You want to make sure you're able to track them regularly instead of looking at a whole sheet of semi-important numbers that really make no sense at all.

I recommend you share your critical numbers with your team and even create a visual representation in your office of what you are tracking. In our office, we have a whiteboard with the quarterly target up the top and a monthly breakdown underneath. We update this daily. Other business owners might build a rocket with their goal up at the pointy end or have their numbers up in lights. Involve your team and have fun with it. It means you're not the only one responsible for (and stressed about) the numbers and the end goal. It also means you're not the one finding the numbers as well as the solutions. At our daily huddle, the receptionist finds our sales number and writes it on the whiteboard. If we're struggling with reaching our targets, our weekly meetings are then a great place to brainstorm things we can do to make sure we stay on track. Lots of heads thinking of creative ideas for your business are always better than one.

The most important thing to do is set goals, work out your critical numbers and track them regularly. Will you get your numbers wrong sometimes? Absolutely. Will there be other numbers you could be tracking that are more important? Maybe. You won't know until you start.

Walking out of your house feeling confident and fabulous is great, but if you arrive at your destination soaking wet and freezing cold then you're probably going to want to give up early and go home. The same is true in your business. Protect yourself and your business by donning your trench and tracking the critical numbers that will make arriving at your destination more comfortable and mean you'll have a whole lot more fun when you get there.

to-do list

1. write down up to three critical numbers for your business.
2. work out the target and tracking period (e.g. 1 july through to 30 september) for each critical number.
3. share the numbers with your team, put them up in your office and get started.

shopping list

- [ ] how to calculate and find your critical numbers
- [ ] critical numbers for industries
- [ ] action plan for critical numbers

"success is often achieved by those who don't know that failure is inevitable."

Coco Chanel

BUSINESS BASICS:

accessories & the power of small changes

i have always loved jewellery.

Of course I lust after the real thing but I'm also a big fan of costume jewellery. I love oversized cocktail rings, long pearl strands, cuffs and bold necklaces. Being a bit taller, I need to wear chunky statement pieces as dainty accessories just look lost. However, I'm not the type who can do earrings, necklaces, bangles and rings all piled on at once. Instead, I follow the Coco Chanel mantra of removing one thing as you walk out the door. Better to have less and have it be fabulous than confuse the eye with too much.

What I do love is the impact of a single piece of statement jewellery – the absolute drama of a bold, yellow Tom Binns necklace, a colourful, chunky YSL ring or a cheeky, brass Fleur Wood bird-shaped cuff. It's amazing how something so small can change the look and feel of an outfit so dramatically.

How boring life would be without a bit of bling in it!

I think small changes made within a business can also have a dramatic impact. By this, I mean the tweaks and adjustments you make within your business on a semi-regular basis. Often business owners think they need to make big, sweeping changes, but small, regular changes can have an enormous impact. And unlike a large change, it won't leave your team and customers reeling.

What do I mean by this? Well let's look at three small changes you could make in your business. (Not unlike donning a couple of cocktail rings and a great pair of earrings.) We'll choose sales, stock on hand

and debtors (people who owe you money). What if we made little tweaks so each of these three things changed by no more than 5%? Think it's not worth it? Well let me surprise you.

Let's assume the business has sales of $250,000, stock on hand of $50,000 and debtors of $25,000. What would be the impact if you increased sales by 3%, reduced stock on hand by 5% and reduced the amount of money people owed you by 2%? They all sound like tiny numbers and you might think this is not worth your time and effort, but let's look at the result.

If you increase your sales by 3% this means an extra $7,500. If you reduce stock on hand by 5% it's an extra $2,500. If you encourage debtors to pay you quicker it's another $500. All these seem like small numbers, but add them together and it's $10,500 in your bank account for simply making a few tweaks. And here's the great thing – it should cost you absolutely nothing more to have this extra money in your bank account. Now $10,500 can buy you quite a few pairs of shoes!

Initially you may look at your business and decide you need a whole lot of courage. You've been undercharging for a long time, you need to hike your prices up by 25% and you know that nine out of 10 clients will be OK with that. Perfect. But once you've increased the price it's time to work out where you can accessorise. Work out the three areas in your business where you can make small tweaks so you too can make sure you are getting the most out of your business (and increasing the size of your bank account).

Once you've made these changes, the idea is not to sit back and rest on your laurels. It might take you three months to make the changes, implement the new policies and ensure your team are running with the new procedures. But once that's done you need to start looking for the next areas you can tweak. Maybe you can reduce your stationery costs by 2% by going paperless or your labour costs by 3% by looking at some internal efficiencies or produce an extra 4% of your product by implementing a new procedure. None of these numbers sound particularly exciting on their own, but group them together and they have a dramatic impact.

I'm a great believer in small changes having a positive impact on your business as it has worked incredibly well in my own business. It simply involves you and your team adopting a mindset of seeking ways you can constantly improve what you are doing.

You may already be thinking of small ways you can make changes in your business – that's fantastic. My advice is to simply start doing it. You don't buy gorgeous accessories and then place them lovingly in your jewellery box and never wear them. (Hopefully not, anyway.) Instead, start picking out three areas at a time where you can make small changes, test them and then see whether the changes worked. Once you're confident that everything is working well, move on to the next three.

Don't be put off by the small numbers. Small changes are like a fantastic cocktail ring. Sure, it might not look like much on its own, but when worn with the right outfit and oodles of confidence it's the statement piece that pulls the outfit together.

to-do list

1. write down up to three areas where you can make small changes in your business.
2. work out the amount of change you want to achieve (e.g. dollars or percentage).
3. write down a strategy for achieving this change.
4. work out a start date and end date.

shopping list

- ☐ table demonstrating power of small changes
- ☐ action plan for small changes

GROOMING: HOW OFTEN DO YOU MAINTAIN?

my husband and i have very different grooming routines.

His involves applying sunscreen every morning, shaving his face most nights, shaving his head once a fortnight and the occasional removal of ear and nose hair. This last one would occur weekly if I had my way, but sadly I don't.

Mine is a little different… OK I'm just going to take a deep breath and spit it all out. I moisturise my face and neck morning and night plus apply extra serums of an evening, moisturise the rest of my body every morning, apply make-up daily, run the straightener through my hair daily, cleanse my face every evening, shower morning and night, shave weekly (laser has eliminated the need for that to occur more often, thank goodness), attack and apply nail polish to my toenails fortnightly, go to the hairdressers weekly for a blow-dry and every two months for a colour, pluck the stray eyebrow hairs when I see them, bikini wax every second month and apply fake tan weekly during summer. Phew. It was exhausting just writing it all down.

I know there are many women out there who do a whole lot less (and have probably shown their partner this chapter and he's now holding them close) and others who do a whole lot more. The point is, hopefully you have some sort of regular grooming routine that, for the most part, you don't think about. It's just habit.

I also have a grooming routine for my business to make sure it's looking its best. The routine includes a daily stand up huddle with the whole team at 9:09 am, admin and bookkeeping department meetings on Tuesday mornings, Lunch and Learn with the team on Fridays, fortnightly accountants' in-house technical training, monthly management meetings, monthly budget update and reporting, monthly meeting with the PR/marketing team, quarterly planning days with the entire team to roll out the next quarter's plan and work out what worked and what didn't for the last quarter, quarterly sessions with my coaching group and bi-annual time out for a few days at the start of each January and July to think and plan for the next six months.

In a four week cycle, that means we have 37 meetings (or 39 if it's the end of a quarter). That sounds like a ridiculous amount, doesn't it? But I know through trial and error that whether it's a nine minute daily huddle or a quarterly planning day, each part of this grooming routine is essential for the health of my business. It wouldn't be as healthy and vibrant if we removed one of the steps.

Now I know some of you are groaning because you hate meetings. So do I. Really! The problem is, putting aside regular time to meet either with yourself or your team is too important. So it means you simply need to have them. The type of meeting though and the time spent at them is critical. In the same way it doesn't take three hours for my hairdresser to blow-dry my hair, our meetings also don't run on for hours. Instead, they're short, sharp and always have an agenda. For example, our daily stand up huddle is no longer than nine minutes and my monthly budget update takes no more than an hour.

Could we survive as a business if we removed a meeting? Of course we could. If I stopped our 50-minute Lunch and Learn every Friday we could still operate and still be profitable. But during this meeting we review the commitments each team member has made that quarter,

I check in to see how everyone is doing and for 20 minutes they receive training on an area of business I want them to focus on. This means I can adapt their individual training if they're not meeting their commitments or solve a minor issue before it becomes a fatal flaw. It has also allowed us to watch Ted Talks, read books together and have time to work on issues as they arise. It's proactive grooming rather than reactive.

The nature of your routine will be unique to your business but just like everyone should shower every day, there are some things you need to do regularly. I think every business needs a daily update of their critical number/s, daily workflow update, weekly department meetings, monthly budget meetings, monthly management meetings and quarterly planning time. You might add in extras or you might disagree with some of these. The most important thing is you're undergoing regular maintenance within your business and not just hoping that no one will notice the smell that is starting to waft from your business because it's not having a regular shower.

Now the most important part of any grooming routine is that you actually do it. Regularly. That involves discipline. Discipline is probably the least sexy piece of advice I give to my clients but it's also one of the most important. What if I decided I was tired of showering and I was only going to start doing it once a week because it took up too much time and money? Or that it was exhausting applying my make-up every day so I wasn't going to wash it off and instead try to make it last an extra day? Firstly, my husband would instantly veto either suggestion but it also wouldn't work for me. Ever. There are some things that simply need to happen more regularly.

The same is true within your business. The un-sexy part of being a business owner is the routine you need to implement to make sure you're running the best business possible. You need to determine which routines you need, how often you're going to do them and schedule them into your diary. Then stick to them!

When you get busy it will be tempting to skip steps in your routine. Don't. The most important part of your grooming routine is the regularity. Sure, there might be some steps you can delay for a few days in the same way you might push back a waxing appointment by a week, but make sure you always delay rather than cancel.

I find discipline to be one of the hardest parts of running my business. Sometimes I simply don't feel like holding a meeting or running a planning day or training my team. My advice to myself when I feel like that is simply 'suck it up and do it'. That's the same advice I give to you. Grooming can be monotonous and boring but there's always a basic level you need to maintain. The amount of grooming you do will depend on how polished you want your business to be. Decide, schedule it and then simply have the discipline to maintain until you don't even notice you're doing it anymore. That's how discipline becomes habit and how before you know it, you discover you're a fan of meetings now too.

to-do list

1. write down the meetings and regular reviews (with your team, with your board, with coaches and with yourself) you're currently holding within your business.

2. decide which meetings are necessary and which are not serving a purpose.

3. write down the meetings or reviews that are missing within your business.

4. create a schedule of meetings and reviews (including the actual day of the month/year and the regularity of them) and an agenda for each one.

5. put the dates in your diary, pick a date to start and then start your grooming routine.

shopping list

- [ ] fact sheet on the daily huddle
- [ ] video links to the daily huddle
- [ ] agenda for a weekly lunch and learn
- [ ] action plan for your business routine

SHOES, MOTIVATION AND MENTORS

i'm not sure when my love affair with shoes began. I've been 5"10 since I was 12 years old. That's right, almost six feet tall since before I was a teenager. Now I'm not sure if you remember how desperate you were to fit in when you were a teenager, but being an awkward, freckly, tall girl did not work well for me in my developmental years. Thankfully, I had a gorgeous Nana who was also tall, which was highly unusual for a woman of her age. She used to encourage me to stand up straight and enjoy the ability to look down at people. She also sent my sister and I pictures of tall, beautiful models in magazines to inspire us. It makes me smile just thinking about her.

Thankfully in my 20s I joined an incredibly supportive state league netball team and, as I played defence, I found myself in the unusual position of being a little too short. So I started to stand straighter and enjoy the fact I was no longer the one who stood a head taller than everyone else. As my confidence grew, I also started to wear the smallest of kitten heels.

Fast forward 10 years and 5-inch heels are de rigour. My husband brags I could win a 100m sprint in a pair of heels and I'm quietly confident he's right. Of course, I didn't jump from kitten heels to 5-inch stilettos overnight. It was a gradual progression. Now I call anything less than 3-inches flats and I'm sure I'm going to make a foot surgeon very wealthy one day.

So what does my obsession with shoes have to do with your business?

Firstly, I think it's important to have motivation and to reward yourself when you've done well in your business. Being a business owner is tough and there are times when you wonder if the hours and the stress are worth it. Your reward may not be the thing that motivates you but it may be the carrot that keeps you going when you encounter something outside your comfort zone. Shoes have always been my great motivator. For you it might be weekends away, handbags, artwork or a massage. Whatever it is, make sure you work out your own personal carrot and reward yourself when you reach a milestone in your business.

It's so easy to just move onto the next thing (because there's always a next thing) but make sure you take a moment and acknowledge you made it. Maybe you achieved the annual sales goal, won the big account or sold your 10,000th unit of product. For me, it's really important to celebrate with my team but I also believe you need to acknowledge and reward your success as the business owner.

Secondly, I believe it's important to have mentors in business. But what does that have to do with shoes? Well, just like I had incredible women in my personal life who helped me embrace my height and ultimately a 5-inch stiletto, you need to find these people in the business arena.

I know firsthand that business can be isolating. Especially if you're a solo operator. At times you will feel exactly as I did at age 12, standing 3-inches above the rest of my classmates - exposed, stressed and very alone. That's why it's important to have key people you trust who can support and encourage you as a business owner. I was fortunate to start my business at the same time as two incredible women, Debbie O'Connor from White River Design and Andrea Turner-Boys who now runs The Fruit Tree Boutique. These women have been unofficial mentors to me throughout the 10 years I've been in business. Debbie loves to tell the story of our first meeting when I was so shy I could barely squeak out my name, never mind what I did. These two women took me under their wing, introduced me to other business owners and gave me confidence. I'm eternally thankful to have met them both.

I'm also blessed to have two mentors within my own family. Firstly my incredibly supportive husband who's in business himself and so understands the pressures of being a business owner. He's my greatest cheerleader and believes in what I'm doing sometimes more than I do. But he also pulls me up when I take on a little too much… which is often. You need someone on your team who will do this for you too. Someone who will wave the pom poms but also pull on the brake. Finally, my dad owned a successful business for 25 years and has acted as a sounding board for me throughout the years, particularly when I first started in business. I feel very fortunate to have these two incredible men in my corner.

So, how do you find a mentor? It's easy – just ask someone.

You might be part of a networking group where a few of you can meet to support one another. Or maybe there's a business owner you admire – try approaching them and asking if they're willing to meet with you. This can simply be via phone if you're both time-poor or a distance away. Your mentor doesn't need to be another business owner although I think this helps. They might be a coach, consultant, accountant or simply a good friend – as long as you trust they will tell you what you need to hear and not simply what you want to hear. For me, that's the key.

I sometimes think back to who I was when I first started business. The painfully shy 29-year-old who just wanted to start something on the side to support more study. Thankfully I have grown and developed over time. The person I am today and the business I have is a testament to my own tenacity, a great team, my ability to implement and my willingness to learn. But it's also thanks in no small part to those people who have guided and supported me along the way.

I'm thankful to those people in my life who have given me the confidence to stride out in my 5-inch heels with my head held high and shoulders thrown back. I encourage you to find mentors who can do the same for you. Of course, once they've encouraged you and supported you to achieve your own business goals, don't forget to reward yourself with a pair of fabulous shoes. Or whatever your own carrot is.

to-do list

1. if you don't already reward yourself, choose a quarterly reward and align it with a business goal.

2. if you don't already have a business mentor, make a list of potential mentors and approach them. once you have secured a mentor set up regular dates to meet and put them in your diary.

shopping list

- [ ] action plan for rewards
- [ ] action plan for mentors

"give a girl the right shoes, and she can conquer the world."

Marilyn Monroe

HOW TO WEAR A HAT

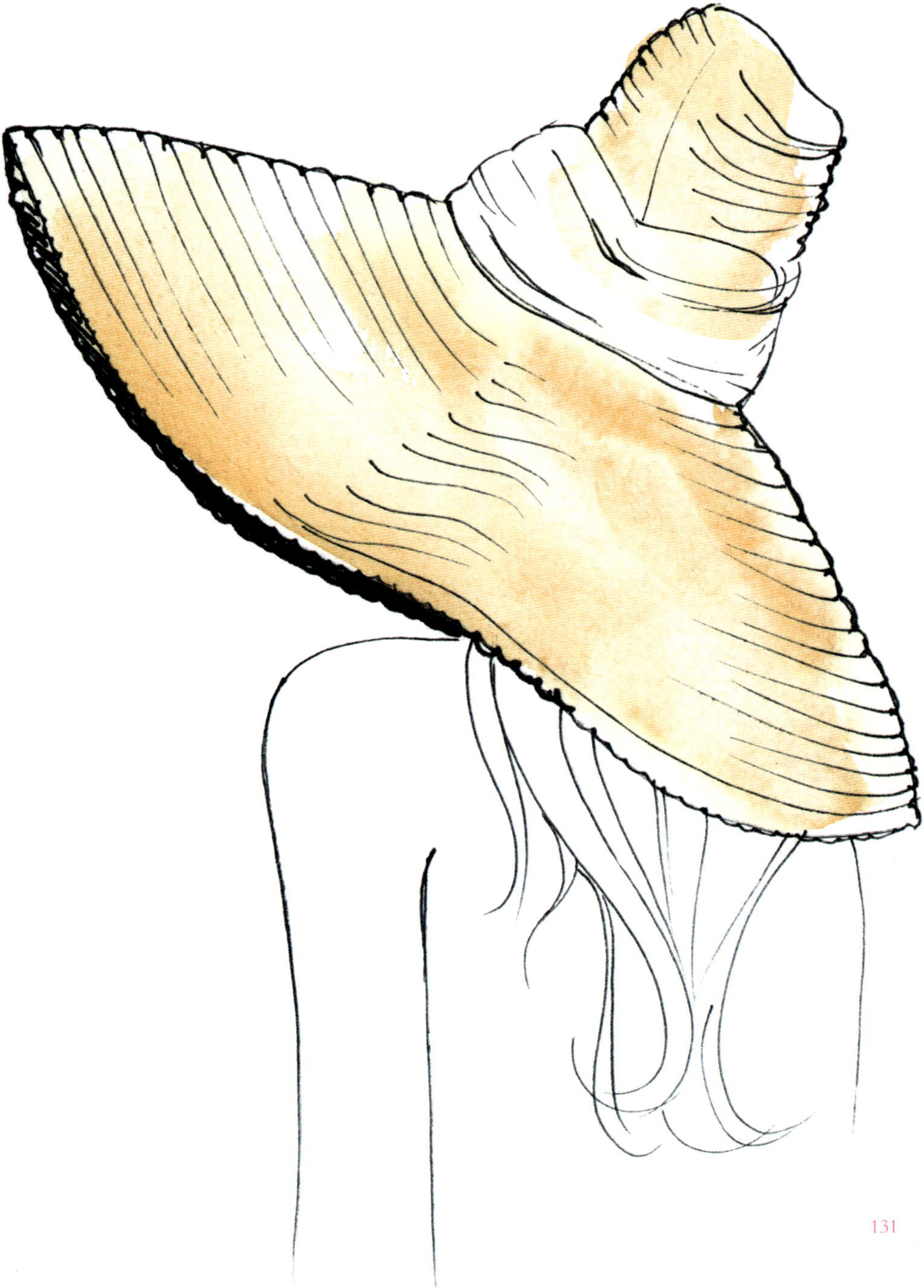

being a business owner can be tough. You have to wear a lot of hats, especially initially, and some of those hats just won't feel comfortable or suit you. But I have something to tell you that I think you might already suspect: sometimes you simply don't have a choice.

As for me, I can't wear a baseball cap. It just feels wrong and looks wrong on me. I much prefer a big, floppy, white, broad-brimmed sun hat.

In my business though, I have a baseball cap that I have to wear. That baseball cap is networking. When I first started out more than 10 years ago I detested networking – actually loathed it. It felt like a big, polyester, brightly coloured, wide-brimmed baseball cap on my head and I did not want to wear it. The problem was I had to do it in order to promote my business. So instead of refusing to wear the baseball cap, I shortened the brim, found a colour I could work with and tried to rock what I had.

How? Well, initially I found an amazing local women's networking group called Women with Altitude. This encouraging environment gave me the confidence to step into other networking groups, knowing firstly I could do it and secondly there were other women who supported me. I also went to seminars and workshops, which gave me tools to use when I went to networking events. I learnt things like perfecting my elevator speech and the importance of listening to someone, asking questions, being interested and not trying to sell yourself. It was such a relief to know I could simply turn up with the attitude of finding out about someone else or wanting to introduce myself to a particular person and find out more about them. The focus shifted from me and as I met more business owners through networking, I found I would pick up tips, find suppliers, find potential customers for my clients, give advice and, most importantly, still pick up clients for myself. All through a change of attitude.

Nowdays I still find networking an uncomfortable fit but I like to think I'm much better at it. I still gravitate towards women's networking groups like the Little Black Dress Group, Business Chicks and Women with Altitude, but I can now strap on my baseball cap and confidently turn up to other networking events too. The difference is, instead of trying to make myself unnaturally fit the cap by wearing a blue suit and trying to look like what an accountant is supposed to look like, I wear what I feel comfortable in. I also chat, laugh, talk about shoes and happily and confidently engage in discussions about business. That's because I'm confident in what my business has to offer and my success as a business owner, so I don't have to look and act like every other accountant on the block. In fact, I've learned to use the fact that I'm a tall, blonde female with a penchant for high, bright shoes to my advantage.

Every business owner has a hat they don't want to wear. For you, maybe it's budgeting, managing staff or strategic planning. So do you have a toddler tantrum, throw the hat in the bin and refuse to wear it? Or instead do you try and find a way to work with it and, when the business can afford it, give that cap away to someone who can rock it much better than you can? Like me, you need to work out which hats you don't enjoy wearing in your business (or don't want to wear) and then work out a plan for how you are going to manage them so your business doesn't suffer.

The bad news is your business can't afford your tantrum. So decide to modify the hat you're uncomfortable with, get skilled up on how to make it work for you and then if you can down the track, offload it to someone else. Eventually the hats you have to wear will reduce but the skills you pick up from wearing them will be invaluable. Who knows, like me, you might even find a hat you once loathed grows on you.

to-do list

1. list the areas in your business you don't feel comfortable with.
2. work out a plan for how you are going to master each of these areas.
3. put dates around your plan, book any seminars/workshops/experts you need to call in to help you and get started.

shopping list

- [ ] action plan for reworking your hat

HOW TO WORK A TREND

i am a fashion magpie. I confess while I love the classics, whenever a trend appears I'm distracted by the latest bright, shiny thing and try to adapt it into my wardrobe. Sometimes that works and, looking back through photos, sometimes it really doesn't. (Note to self: stonewashed denim is always wrong.)

While following trends can be fun, you need to know how to adapt the trend to your style. For example, I would feel so very wrong wearing tight, coloured jeans with bright shoes and a coloured top, yet a 21-year-old would look perfect in it. But I can adapt the fluoro look by wearing one piece at a time. So a fluorescent yellow silk top with tailored pants or perhaps some fluoro shoes with a pair of cuffed jeans are perfect.

It would also cost way too much to follow every trend and that takes money away from my shoe budget. (And that's never OK.)

In business you can also be distracted, and bankrupted, by the many trends and fads that come along. At the moment social media is a huge trend. Do you Tweet, do you have a Facebook page, a LinkedIn profile or are you pinning on Pinterest? Are you YouTubing, blogging or Tumblring? If you chase the latest bright shiny thing in the social media world, you'll end up spending all of your time on social media and not doing any of the actual work.

So how do you adapt the social media trend to your business?

Firstly, you need to work out which social media platforms are most appropriate to your business. How do you do that? Hopefully by now you've worked out who your customers are and where they hang out. So if you're looking for a 50-year-old male you may not find him on Twitter (or any social media platform at all), but if your target market is new mums then you might find them on Facebook.

Your type of business will also dictate which social media platform you use. My business is an information business (accounting and business coaching) so I use social media to interact with clients and potential clients, but also to deliver information. I find Twitter, Facebook and LinkedIn are best for that. If you're in a creative industry such as interior design or publishing, then Twitter, Instagram and Pinterest may be preferable so you can display images and let potential customers know your style. Just don't jump onto a platform because that's where everyone is telling you to be. You need to do your homework first.

Once you've worked out your appropriate social media platforms, you need to work out a strategy for each. That means asking questions such as:

- How will you interact in that space?
- Who are you trying to reach – clients, potential clients or media?
- How many times a day will you post/Tweet/Tumblr/blog?
- How many hours are you prepared to dedicate each week?
- How many followers do you want?

Next, you need to work out what you're going to say and how you're going to say it. Decide what message you want to get across, but make sure it isn't selling because the quickest way to alienate followers on social media is to try to sell them something. Instead, social media is about engaging with your customers and potential customers. For example, my business uses Twitter and Facebook to tell people what we're doing, share news items we've seen that we think are useful, give tax and business tips, ask questions, post pictures, share clients' success stories and comment on their posts, engage with other people we think are interesting and share links to newsletters and blog posts. What isn't included in this list? We're not actively selling anything.

We also don't sound like accountants when we use social media. The platforms we use have an informal tone, so to jump on and start lecturing people in an academic style would be alienating. Instead, our tone is conversational – almost like I'm sitting opposite you having a chat. You need to look at the tone of the platforms you want to use and work out what your own style and tone will be on those sites.

The next question to ask yourself is how often will you use your social media platforms? You might blog weekly, update LinkedIn fortnightly, post on Facebook daily and Tweet half a dozen times each day. If you think that sounds like a lot to cope with, the good news is there are programs available to help you manage your posts. Programs such as TweetDeck and HootSuite allow you to schedule multiple posts, which means you can spend a chunk of time at the start of the week or month setting it up and then you simply set and forget. Of course, you still need to jump on and monitor who is commenting, re-Tweeting, liking and sharing. You also want to engage regularly with users of these social media platforms and not just talk at people. No one likes someone who simply talks and doesn't listen and respond.

The final step is the one loved by accountants everywhere: testing and measuring. You might think you look fab in your big-shouldered, floral suit but when you look at photos afterwards you know it just doesn't work. The same goes for social media. Maybe you'll start with Facebook, Twitter and Pinterest and then work out that Pinterest isn't working for you, so you move on to LinkedIn instead. Or perhaps certain posts are generating a lot of interest but others fall flat. You need to adjust your message to suit what your audience is responding to. The most important thing is to understand the platform, use it consistently and measure what is happening.

Once you know what platforms you want to use then jump on and see what other businesses are doing. For example, companies such as Supré, Sportsgirl and Lorna Jane engage incredibly well with their customers on Facebook. Sportsgirl has taken things a step further by installing interactive mirrors in their stores so their customers can upload straight to Facebook. Of course it's also important to understand your market and what your customers are thinking. In 2011 Qantas started a Twitter campaign that backfired when customers, annoyed by the strikes, used the hashtag to vent their frustration publicly. It's an example of how not to engage with your customers, particularly if you have just annoyed them. If you want to know more then head to the case studies in the Shopping List below.

Last of all, have fun. Life is too short not to play with fads, especially when there's no cost (other than your time) and your customers and potential customers are already there waiting for you. Just make sure everything you do on social media is an extension of your brand and doesn't conflict with the message you're already sending.

What do you have to lose? So pull on that jumpsuit, step into those platform shoes and have fun trying on a few different business trends to see what works best for you.

to-do list

1. write down your potential customer types (you should already have completed this).
2. write underneath each customer type what social media platform they're likely to use.
3. write down the social media platforms that will best suit your business.
4. align points two and three above.
5. develop a strategy for each platform, taking into account your answers above.
6. work out what you're going to say.
7. find the tools you're going to use to help manage your social media usage.
8. get started by setting up pages, accounts etc. and then pick a date to start communicating.

shopping list

- ☐ table comparing different social media platforms
- ☐ social media marketing plan
- ☐ case studies on social media (good and bad)

THE HEAD-TURNERS: YOUR VALUES & PURPOSE

one of my favourite things to do is sit somewhere and watch people walk by. Whether it's sitting at a café, at the airport or at a park, I love people watching.

What I've noticed over time is a beautifully styled man or woman will often turn my head, but it's the confident man or woman who fascinates me. This confidence is obvious in the way they move – with poise and assuredness. It's not the swagger of a teenager but the attractiveness of someone who knows their style and is sure of themselves within it. They're not necessarily the most attractive person (in fact, they very rarely are) but there's something absolutely captivating about them. This confidence comes from within and is so much more interesting than beauty.

Now confidence, poise and self-assuredness are not things you can buy off the shelf. They're all internal qualities. You can't put on a dress and be confident. Sure, wearing the dress may make you feel confident but it's not something extra you gain when you purchase it. Instead, it's something you develop. For me, a great outfit is nonsensical without confidence. You don't notice the clothes if someone is stooping, fidgeting and looks like they aren't comfortable in them.

I believe in business there are also some internal qualities that will make your business incredibly attractive to an onlooker. A head-turner, if you like.

I'm not talking about business confidence or bravado here, Instead, I'm talking about the internal business qualities that will make your business incredibly attractive to your team and your customers. The internal qualities that, just like those with inner poise and assuredness captivate me as they walk by, will set your business apart from the crowd.

What inner qualities am I talking about? Your business' core values and purpose.

Now I don't mean a mission statement you write up one day, stick on an office wall and forget about. Instead, your values are the things that define how your business will operate. They announce to the world what's important to your business. You may already know these in your head but I believe it's important to write them down, put them up (we have them at every person's desk on our quarterly plan) and then revisit them regularly. That's because these are the things that are going to make your business stand out as attractive to someone that is sitting and watching.

Need inspiration? In my business, our core values and beliefs are:

1. Intimacy: We take the time to get to know our customers and earn their trust.
2. Transparency: We are honest, upfront and courageous with each other and our clients.
3. Reliability: We do what we say we're going to do and we do it well.
4. Credibility: We earn the right to advise our clients on their business by being the best business we can be.
5. Embracing the fear: The fear of losing business, being embarrassed or being inferior.
6. Giving back: With our time and our money.

If someone in my business (including me) is not acting within these core values then anyone in my team has the right to address them on their behaviour. Our core values also explain the way my team and I act, look and speak. For example, I'm keenly aware some people might be put off by the 'too much information' shared by me throughout this book. I've actually contemplated stripping a lot of it out. But if I did the message I wanted to get across – if I can do this then you certainly can – would be lost. In other words, I'm living out values two and five. I've written authentically because I know if you were sitting across from me, I may at some point have all of the same conversations I've had with you in this book. If I can make a point or help you understand something then I don't mind using examples that are a little unusual or personal.

The second internal quality I believe that can really set a business apart is their core purpose. Simon Sinek, the uber business stylist, calls this finding your 'why'. I think this one word explains it beautifully. Your business' 'why' is the thing that gets you out of bed as a business owner and makes you want to do more for your customers and team – and I'm not talking about money. It's the thing you're left with when you keep asking yourself why you do what you do. For example, Disney's 'why' is to make people happy. It's simple and it's immediately clear to their suppliers, their team and their customers what they're all about.

My business' 'why' is to change our peoples' lives. Our people are my team, our clients and the families and communities that are attached to them. We funnel all our products, services and team members through our 'why' and if they don't fit, then it doesn't matter how great the idea is or how great the person's skills are, they simply can't be a match for our business.

When I understood and articulated my business' 'why' and core values, it became easier for my team and I to make decisions on what happened within the business. Suddenly everything was not up to me to decide because if my team and I funnelled what we're doing through the core values and the 'why' then some decisions were made automatically. Of course, this hasn't necessarily made things easier for me as a business owner. Staying true to our 'why' and core values has meant moving on a team member, moving on a client and changing how we offered our services. These aren't always easy things to do. But if you're going to have a values-driven business then at times you're going to have to make some tough decisions.

Our 'why' and values define the reason I'm in business. Sure, I always knew in my head I wanted my business to be all about my clients and I tried to impart this to my team. But when I was able to clearly and simply articulate why, they suddenly grasped why this was important. They understood the reason behind why we did things. It's now crystal clear to my team why the business exists and why we do things the way we do. They don't question a process if they can see it fulfils our core purpose. They just do it. I've found it's not only my three-year-old nephew who needs his 'why' to be answered. As adults, we need it answered too.

Now some of you might argue money is your reason to be in business – your 'why'. But trust me, the motivation of money will eventually fade and you'll need a better reason to keep pushing. Wanting to make money will (and should) always be a business goal, but you as the business owner need something other than money to motivate your clients and your team to be with you. As corny as it sounds, they need a purpose. People want to be a part of something they believe in and with your 'why' and core values you can begin to create that.

Without a 'why' and core values, your business may still deliver a great product or service, have a great time and deliver you a profit you're happy with. But I don't believe that kind of business will ever be a head-turner. If you're going to build a business, style it beautifully and spend time making sure it's running smoothly, then why not spend that extra time creating a business that is not just well put together, but is captivating, too?

Defining the purpose of my business has literally changed how I do business on a daily basis – for the better. I challenge you to create a business with values and purpose, too. Then have the courage to live those values and that purpose through your business on a daily basis.

to-do list

1. if you already have core values and a 'why' (purpose) then dust them off and review them. are they still relevant? are they still meaningful?
2. if you don't have these then spend some time creating them (include your team in this if you can).
3. share your core values and 'why' with your team, put it on your website and revisit them often.

shopping list

- [ ] how to find your 'why'
- [ ] how to develop your core values and beliefs

RESOLUTIONS V GOALS

i don't do new year's resolutions.

Maybe it's because I'm a perpetual planner that I find them a little bit twee. Plus, there's the fact they're usually made while completely tanked or in the grip of a raging hangover the next day. Either way, I don't believe it's a real recipe for success.

Of course just because I'm a resolution knocker, doesn't mean I don't applaud goal setting. Some goals, like committing to wear more jumpsuits, discarding tracksuits, being able to pay yourself a regular wage in your business, or world peace are worthy goals and should be taken seriously. It's what you do once you have a vague notion of a goal that's important.

So if you've read this book and are inspired to become a better business owner (or perhaps to start a business) then here are some steps to turn that wish into reality...

1. Is your goal specific and measurable? Wearing jumpsuits more often or making more money in your business is too wishy-washy. Wearing a jumpsuit every calendar month or paying yourself a weekly wage of $1,000 can be tracked.

2. Does your goal get your juices flowing? If you aren't inspired to achieve your goal, you won't bother, so make sure you're emotionally invested. For me, a goal to run a marathon would make me want to run a mile (sorry, couldn't help myself). However, a goal to achieve sales of $1 million in my business by the end of the 2013 financial

year or to wear dresses every day for the month of December inspires me.

3. What steps do you need to take to achieve your goal? A fanciful idea is not a goal, so you need to sort out the steps you need to take to make it happen. This doesn't need to be a 100-page prospectus. Instead, a to do list or a notes page on your computer or phone (if you're a little more tech savvy) with a few steps is usually enough to get you started.

4. Is your goal realistic? If I'm 5"10 and my goal is to be 6"2, then it's probably not going to happen (except with the help of a great pair of heels). Similarly, if your goal is to make sales of $1 million and you're currently at $5,000, maybe you need to sit down and do the maths to see if it's achievable. Of course, a stretch target is great – just make sure it's within the realm of probability.

5. When is your deadline? Are you going to achieve success with your goals in a month, a quarter, six months, a year? Set a date by which you'll achieve your goal and mark it on your calendar.

6. Tell people. Nothing makes you take action like telling people you're going to do something. Tell your partner, family, friends, colleagues, social media or blog about it. Then keep these people updated with how you're going.

Now the only thing missing is the reward. That's because if you're going to put in all of this effort then I think you need to plan a reward for yourself. For me, unsurprisingly, the reward is usually shoes. You might be different. Find your carrot and then, to use the words of a modern-day philosopher, "just do it".

to-do list

1. if you have already created your resolutions and goals then revisit them to see if they need to be tweaked, using this chapter as a guide.

2. if you haven't set your resolutions and goals then take the time to write them now.

3. you might have new goals after reading this book, like implementing workflow processes, taking a holiday or implementing systems. set these goals using the guide above.

shopping list

- [ ] smart goals checklist
- [ ] action plan template
- [ ] action plan for goal setting

A FINAL WORD: BE EXTRAORDINARY

on my second wedding anniversary, I organised a romantic weekend in Sydney at the Observatory Hotel with dinner at the Galileo restaurant. All very swish. So of course, as I love dressing up, I thought it was a fantastic excuse to buy a red, corseted Alex Perry number. Very glamorous. Also a little bit over the top. But that's never really bothered me before so why start now? That is, until the week before the anniversary when I tried on the dress to make sure it still worked.

That's when I realised my dress was extraordinary.

Now I knew this prior to trying it on. I mean it was a red, satin, corseted Alex Perry number with three layers on the skirt (did I miss that bit out before?). Not the kind of thing you'd pop down to the shops in, but standing in my dress I knew it would be extraordinary. I'm talking about the dress, not me. Trust me, this dress was that good.

So what did I do? I grabbed a safe LBD, styled it up and figured I would take it with me as a back up. Just in case I couldn't face the 'extraordinary' dress.

Ridiculous, isn't it? Firstly, I'm sure most men are exhausted at this point, but what is truly ridiculous is to buy the most fabulous dress and then not want to wear it because it's too fabulous.

What occurred to me through that experience was my internal struggle that weekend was one many business owners go through every day. Not to choose between dresses, but to choose between being safe and being extraordinary. You might think that's a crazy thing to say – of course business owners would want to be extraordinary! But do they really? As Australians, I think we're taught to cut tall poppies down – to stay just below the stellar line and fit in.

Being extraordinary means putting yourself out there, taking a risk and having the spotlight shine on you and what you're doing. It might mean having to look at areas of your business you're not comfortable with, like budgets, business plans, branding or systems. Or sharing your goals and being held accountable. Or maybe taking a risk and having a go at something you've been telling yourself you'll never understand, like the numbers. Or borrowing from the bank or an angel investor to take your business to the next level. Or not being afraid to say you want to be fabulously successful.

In the end, I wore my ridiculously fantastic dress. My husband was pleasantly surprised (but also a little shocked) when he saw me. But trust me, he'll remember that dress.

Life is too short to play it safe. You owe it to yourself, as well as your team, your customers and your suppliers, to have an extraordinary business. So decide today to have a real go. To embrace the possibility that hiding within you is an extraordinary business owner. Your business has the potential to be an incredible success if you allow yourself to know it's OK for you to want to chase that.

Take a deep breath and make the decision to have a business that is successful, profitable, unique, fabulous and one that will certainly stand out in the crowd. In short, decide today to be extraordinary.

what comes next

Now that you've read this book, I hope you're inspired to create a business that is profitable, successful and amazing.

Inside you is the potential to be an amazing business person – you just need to start doing the basics. So get cracking on your To Do Lists, head to www.moremoneyforshoes.com.au and start downloading the free tools you marked off in the Shopping Lists and get started!

If it all seems too hard, just take a deep breath and start with one thing at a time. Of course, if you need more help then make sure you check out my websites at the back of the book or contact me to find out about the many ways that my team and I can assist you.

If you loved the book, make sure you pre-register for our webinar series, More Money for Shoes 12-week Business Makeover which starts in 2013. All you need to do is jump on the More Money for Shoes website to pre-enrol. Learning in your pj's – who doesn't love that!

Finally, don't forget to drop me a line and let me know the many ways that you are now making sure that you have more money for shoes in your business.

mel x

acknowledgements

Thank you to the two Laurens (my editor and my senior accountant) for their many read-throughs of the draft manuscript. Thanks also to the very talented Camille Howard for taking a look at the early rough draft and providing invaluable feedback on what it needed.

Thank you to the girls at The Messenger Group who understood my vision for this book immediately and helped turn my crazy idea into reality. Your support and guidance has been amazing.

To the fabulously talented illustrator of this book, Kelly Coates – I am completely in awe of your creativity and style. Thank you for interpreting everything so deliciously.

Finally to my amazing team at ATA who make it possible for me to do what I do, all I can say is thank you – and that I think it's time to crack out the bubbles now.

sometimes in business you need to call in the experts.

To find out more about the many ways that Melissa and her team can work with you to create a successful, profitable business please visit her websites or contact her directly.

Accounting and Taxation Advantage
www.acctaxadv.com.au

Business Advantage Coaching
www.businessadvantagecoaching.com.au

More Money for Shoes
www.moremoneyforshoes.com.au

Melissa Browne
T 1300 692 228
E melissa@acctaxadv.com.au

If you're after a traditional accountant then she's obviously not for you. Instead, if you're after a team that will find opportunities, minimise your tax, help you build wealth, educate, inspire, train, guide, hold you accountable and support you in creating an incredible, successful business, then Melissa and her team may be exactly what you're looking for.

Melissa is a dynamic and engaging speaker who is an expert at removing the bland from understanding the numbers and breaking down how to run a successful and profitable business.